Damsels Arise

Talitha Davis

eBook Edition ISBN-13: 979-8-9893307-1-3

Paperback ISBN-13: 979-8-9893307-2-0

Book Cover by Oneself Design

I dedicate this book to my Lord and Savior Jesus Christ, the One who has kept me through every phase of life. God is truly the reason I stand here today with my head held high with a joy on the inside that never dies. This book has been a labor of love. God helped me to see it through to fruition. It took quite some time to finally write this book and I'm so excited to share this with the world. All I can say is by faith all things are possible. My faith has made me whole!

Dear Reader,

May God bless you richly as you journey through this 12 week devotion. Each day invite God to your heart and get to know Him through His Word. Spending time with the Lord through daily devotion reading helps you apply Biblical principles that will be useful in life. Relying on God's Word and communing with Him through prayer can give you the kind of peace which surpasses all understanding. It gives an unshakable joy in the midst of difficulties.

God desires a relationship with us. He created us and redeemed us for this very purpose. If we desire to truly find rest and safety in God, it is helpful to know Him well. Such a deep knowledge comes from daily time spent with Him. When we expect to meet with Jesus during our quiet time each day, we will never be disappointed. We will always find that He's waiting to meet with us too.

When we sit quietly with the Master, it gives us the opportunity to hear from God and to get the wisdom and direction we need. In our fast paced world, we desperately need to slow down and hear from one who knows the end from the beginning. Ask God to show you His will for your day and commit your schedule to Him.

Contents

Week 1 - Loneliness

Sadness because one has no friends or company; the quality of being unfrequented and remote; isolation

Day 1

<u>Deut. 31:8</u>

Do not be afraid or discouraged, for the Lord will personally go ahead of you. He will be with you; He will neither fail you nor abandon you.

God is omnipresent – ever present always. Just know of times when you are by yourself or alone, you should never feel lonely. Whenever that feeling of loneliness comes upon you, open your mouth, and say, "It is the Lord who is with me right now; He is always by my side wherever I go. He will never leave me or forsake me. Meditate on Deut. 31:8 and let it penetrate your heart and soul. Let this word become apart of you so that you know, without a shadow of doubt, that the Lord is with you always. He sticks closer than a brother. His love for you runs deep like the ocean, and there's no need to fear. For the Lord your God is with you always!

Day 2

Ps. 27:10

Even if my father and mother abandon me, the Lord will hold me close.

This scripture hits deep because I love my mother and father so much. They mean so much to me, and I wouldn't be the woman I am today without them. I thank God for my parents, but even if Mom or Dad left me to never return, the scripture says, "The Lord will take me up." A father is a protector of the family, and a mother is the glue or bond that brings family together. Even in the absence of a protector and the bond of the family, the Lord is saying, *I will receive you to be brought into my family*. God is the supreme protector of us all and to be gathered into His family is a privilege. He loves you so much, and you're received as His own. In times of loneliness, just know this is for the purpose of continuing to seek God. When you seek God, you will find Him, and He will deliver you from all evil.

Day 3

1 Sam. 12:22

The Lord will not abandon His people, because that would dishonor His great name. For it has pleased the Lord to make you His very own people.

The Lord loves you so much, He will never leave you because it pleases Him to make you a people for Himself. The Lord treats those of us who are chosen mercifully for His great name's sake. This is God's biblical principle of divine saving grace or favor. The Lord will not deal with His people according to their wicked deeds. It pleases the Lord to make you His own. He chooses you to come into the fold. You are not alone. Let that sink in and feel the favor of the Lord rest upon you.

Day 4

<u>Rom. 8:37, 39</u>

37 No, despite all these things, overwhelming victory is ours through Christ, who loved us. **38** And I am convinced that nothing can ever separate us from God's love. Neither death nor life, neither angels nor demons,[] neither our fears for today nor our worries about tomorrow—not even the powers of hell can separate us from God's love. **39** No power in the sky above or in the earth below—indeed, nothing in all creation will ever be able to separate us from the love of God that is revealed in Christ Jesus our Lord.

These scriptures say it all! When an overwhelming feeling of loneliness comes upon you, begin to meditate on Rom. 8:37-39 or say it out loud. Yes, speak into the atmosphere. I am more than a conqueror because God turns everything, even loneliness and sorrow, into good. In verse 38, Paul answers the question with absolute certainty that nothing can ever separate or sever God's people from His love in Christ Jesus. This is why it's good to speak the Word of God over your life to serve notice to the ruler, powers, and demonic authorities.

They are defeated and you have the victory in Christ Jesus! Nothing can separate you from His love; just speak the Word of God. Faith comes by hearing and hearing by the word of the Lord. Loneliness is defeated, and all is well in your soul.

Day 5

Matt. 28:20

   Teach these new disciples to obey all the commands I have given you. And be sure of this: I am with you always, even to the end of the age.

   Jesus calls upon His followers to make disciples of all people groups through the preaching of the gospel of the Kingdom of Heaven. It is through His teaching that you are continuously transformed by the renewing of your mind in order to become more like Christ. To observe in the scripture is to "Obey, for I am with you always." Jesus concludes the commission with the crucial element of discipleship; the presence of the master means is "God with us." He's always with you and whenever feeling lonely just remember this scripture. Let it teach you what is true, what is pure, and what is honest. Let this mind that is in me be in Christ Jesus, and let the Word do its perfect work in me. Renew my mind that I will be more like Christ and walking in His resurrection power continuously.

Day 6

<u>Ps. 68:5, 6</u>

5 Father to the fatherless, defender of widows this is God, whose dwelling is holy.**6** God places the lonely in families; he sets the prisoners free and gives them joy.But he makes the rebellious live in a sun-scorched land.

In times when you're feeling lonely, begin to sing praises unto God. Sing unto the Lord a new song and extol Him; for He is the one true God that comes riding through the wilderness as the King of kings and Lord of lords. Call upon His name and He will answer you. Let Him be the answer to all of your problems. The Lord is your Father, protector, provider, healer, savior, and lover of your soul! Oh, magnify the Lord with me and let us exalt His name together. For I have found a dwelling place in your goodness, O God, you provided for me in my time of need.

Day 7

<u>Prov. 18:24</u>

There are 'friends' who destroy each other, but a real friend sticks closer than a brother.

There is loneliness all around us. Many people feel cut off and isolated from others. Lonely people need friends who will stick close, listen, care, and offer help when it is needed in good times, and bad. It is better to have one such friend than dozens of superficial acquaintances. Jesus Christ is a friend that sticks closer than a brother. If you let Jesus in as your friend, He'll teach you how to become one. You'll begin to look around and find people who need your friendship. Ask God to reveal them to you and then take on the challenge of being a true friend yourself.

Join Talitha for devotional hymn chosen to align with this week's focus by scanning this code.

Week 2 - Depression

More than persistent sadness

Day 1

Phil. 4:8

And now, dear brothers and sisters, one final thing. Fix your thoughts on what is true, and honorable, and right, and pure, and lovely, and admirable. Think about things that are excellent and worthy of praise.

Your thought process determines your outlook on life and results in how you live out your life each and every day. Examine what you are putting into your mind. Replace harmful negative material with positive wholesome and Godly material. Let this mind that is in me be in

Christ Jesus. Paul teaches us in this text to train our minds to focus on thoughts that are true, honorable, righteous, pure, lovely, admirable, excellent, and worthy of praise. What are you watching on TV, what are you reading, and what type of conversations are you entertaining? Ask God to help you fill your mind with good and pure thoughts. Practice every day, you can do this and will never be the same.

Day 2

Phil. 4:13

   For I can do everything through Christ,[] who gives me strength.

   God is more than able to keep you from falling. He is a present help in the time of trouble. Life can often times leave you in a web of despair but just know that you can go to God in prayer and He will give you strength to make it through whatever you are going through. When you are weak, He is strong. Meditate on His Word day and night; let it get deep down into your spirit, heart, and mind. The Word is life! Let the Word give life to your bones. Your perspective and outlook on life will begin to change.

Day 3

John 16:33

I have told you all this so that you may have peace in me. Here on earth you will have many trials and sorrows. But take heart, because I have overcome the world.

There is a war going on within us constantly with hostile forces such as persistent sadness and despair, but the peace of God restrains these hostile forces and gives us comfort in place of conflict. Thanks be to God who is more than able to keep you from falling, so take courage! For weeping may endure for a night, but joy comes in the morning. Despite the inevitable struggles you face, remember you are not alone. Jesus does not abandon us to our struggles. If we remember that the ultimate victory has already been won, we can claim the peace of God in the most troublesome times.

Day 4

2 Cor. 7:10

For the kind of sorrow God wants us to experience leads us away from sin and results in salvation. There's no regret for that kind of sorrow. But worldly sorrow, which lacks repentance, results in spiritual death.

Often times we experience sorrow in our lives. There's Godly sorrow and then there's worldly sorrow. God wants us to experience sorrow which can result in a changed behavior. God allows us to encounter challenging and difficult problems that may cause sorrow or sadness. This can cause us to begin to change in the areas where we need to sincerely evaluate it, and grow from it. Peter's remorse and repentance with Juda's bitterness and act of suicide. Both disowned Christ, but one repented and was restored to faith, the other did not. Many people are sorry for their sin when getting caught. We can respond to hearing criticism with self-pity and self-justification, thinking we don't deserve it. The mature Christian should accept the many problems and hardships to face, and find comfort and joy in the progress of the experience.

Day 5

Ps. 39:12

Hear my prayer, O Lord! Listen to my cries for help! Don't ignore my tears. For I am your guest, a traveler passing through, as my ancestors were before me.

Remember that your redeemer lives. You are redeemed by the blood of the Lamb; bought with a price. Jesus sacrificed His life for us. With great sacrifice comes great reward. We have a right to eternal life with Jesus Christ through salvation. As a child of God you are in this world, but not of this world. Realize that all of us are strangers in this world just like travelers passing through. David recognized that our ultimate home is on the earth (Heaven) with God for eternity. Cast your cares upon the Lord and focus on what you can do to change the way you live. For our time here is temporary, but while our time is short, remember what you do for Christ will last. Set your mind on things above (eternal), not on things on the earth. This perspective should change the way we live for the believer.

Day 6

Ps. 40:1,2

1 I waited patiently for the Lord to help me, and he turned to me and heard my cry. **2** He lifted me out of the pit of despair, out of the mud and the mire. He set my feet on solid ground and steadied me as I walked along.

Waiting on the Lord is not an easy thing to do, but patience in the Lord is a heart's virtue. Daid received at least four benefits from waiting: (1) God lifted him out of despair; (2) God set his feet on solid ground; (3) God steadied him as he walked; (4) God put a new song of praise in his mouth. Often times, we cannot receive blessings unless we go through the trial of waiting. During your waiting, allow God to change you. We normally want God to change our circumstances, but God really wants to change you! So just let Him have His way!

Day 7

Rev. 21:4

He will wipe every tear from their eyes, and there will be no more death or sorrow or crying or pain. All these things are gone forever.

Can you imagine what Heaven is like? God says there will be no more crying or pain, no more death, or sorrow. All these things are gone forever. What a promise! God's Word is true, true fulfillment. Just think about the promises of God and believe what He has promised. No matter what you are going through now, it's not the end all be all. God has the final say, for He is the author and finisher of our faith. We don't know everything, but we know enough to believe that eternity with the Lord will be more wonderful than we could ever imagine.

Join Talitha for devotional hymn chosen to align with this week's focus by scanning this code.

Week 3 - Fear

Painful agitation in the presence of anticipation of danger

Day 1

Isa. 41:10

  Don't be afraid, for I am with you. Don't be discouraged, for I am your God. I will strengthen you and help you. I will hold you up with my victorious right hand.

  Every blood-washed, born-again believer has a responsibility to represent Christ in this world. How do you represent Him? We are known by our faith. You are like a tree planted by the rivers of water. A good tree cannot bear bad fruit, nor can a bad tree bear good fruit. Every tree that bears bad fruit is cut down and thrown into the fire. Be a good tree by loving God and keeping His commandments. One day, God will bring all His people together. We need not fear because God is with us (I am with you); God has established His covenant with us ("I am your God"); and God gives us assurance of His strength, help, and victory over the power of sin and death. Remember the ways God has helped you. Always trust and believe that He will continue to help you.

Day 2

Heb. 13:5, 6

5 Don't love money; be satisfied with what you have. For God has said, "I will never fail you. I will never abandon you." **6** So we can say with confidence, "The Lord is my helper, so I will have no fear. What can mere people do to me?

God is Jehovah Shammah (The Lord is There). We can say this with confidence and boldness because God said it in His Word. His promises are Yes and Amen. So yes all is well in my soul. There is no need to fear. Whether we feel rich or poor, anxiety and insecurity can lead us down a path of taking our eyes off God. Trusting in

God to meet all our needs will dissolve and wash away discontentment. Express thanks to God for what He has provided. A thankful heart unlocks victory in our lives.

Day 3

2 Tim. 1:7

For God has not given us a spirit of fear and timidity, but of power, love, and self-discipline.

The key here is the Holy Spirit that can help us overcome our fear so that we can continue to do the work of God in the earth. He gives us power (the ability is not in our own might, but miraculous power in Christ through the Holy Spirit); love (good will towards others); and a sound mind (a believer must have self control by keeping a cool head and letting go of his or her selfish desires). Let us follow the leading of the Holy Spirit so that your life will more freely display these attributes.

Day 4

John 14:27

I am leaving you with a gift—peace of mind and heart. And the peace I give is a gift the world cannot give. So don't be troubled or afraid.

God's peace gives light to them that sit in darkness and in the shadow of death to guide our feet into the way of peace. Let the peace of God guide your heart and mind because peace and harmony make and keep things safe and prosperous. When fear makes its presence known in your hearts, allow Jesus to sit in the midst, and say unto you, "Peace be unto you." Make way and let the peace of God rule in your hearts, and in your mind may you have quietness with assurance in Christ Jesus.

Day 5

Ps. 27:1

The Lord is my light and my salvation, so why should I be afraid? The Lord is my fortress, protecting me from danger, so why should I tremble?

Fear is the like a dark cloud that comes over us and restrains us from a victorious life which God has promised we should live. Everyone has been a slave to fear at one time or another. But we are more than conquerors through Jesus

Christ. Trust in the Lord with all your heart today. Dismiss the darkness of fear in your life and let us remember that the Lord is our light and our salvation.

Day 6

Ps. 91:1, 2

1 Those who live in the shelter of the Most High will find rest in the shadow of the Almighty. **2** This I declare about the Lord: He alone is my refuge, my place of safety; He is my God, and I trust him.

God is our dwelling place where we can get shelter and protection. You don't have to be afraid when there is sickness or trouble in your midst. God will protect His children through all of life's dangers and fears. Today trade your fears for faith in Him, no matter how hard they may be. Just let go and let God by resting in Him. God wants us to entrust ourselves to His protection and pledging our daily devotion in Him. This is how we acknowledge that He will keep us safe always.

Day 7

Ps. 55:22

Give your burdens to the Lord, and he will take care of you. He will not permit the godly to slip and fall.

God wants us to give all of our burdens to Him. Often times we continue to bear our own burdens even when we pray and give it to God, and say we trust in Him. This is like holding heavy bags during a long train ride. It's unnecessary. Trust that God will sustain you everyday to also carry your cares and burdens.

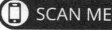

Join Talitha for devotional hymn chosen to align with this week's focus by scanning this code.

Week 4 - Anxiety

A feeling of worry, nervousness, or unease about something with an uncertain outcome

Day 1

Matt. 6:34

So don't worry about tomorrow, for tomorrow will bring its own worries. Today's trouble is enough for today.

Don't worry about tomorrow, because tomorrow is not promised to us. Tiem devoted to planning for tomorrow is time well spent, time devoted to worrying about tomorrow is time wasted. At times it may be difficult to tell the difference. Take joy for today in which

God has given you and make the most of your time today. When you plan carefully thinking ahead about goals and schedules, trusting in God's guidance is key. When done well, it will alleviate worry. Worrying consumes us with anxiety and makes it difficult to trust God. This worrying obsession with plans and outcomes can interfere with your relationship with God. Don't let worries about tomorrow affect your relationship with God.

Day 2

Phil 4:6, 7

6 Don't worry about anything; instead, pray about everything. Tell God what you need and thank him for all he has done. **7** Then you will experience God's peace, which exceeds anything we can understand. His peace will guard your hearts and minds as you live in Christ Jesus.

Have you ever heard of the song "Don't worry, be happy" by Bobby McFerrin? The lyrics are comical, but it definitely makes you stop and think, should I worry about this or just be happy? Do you want to worry less? The answer is pray more! Prayer is the antidote for worry.

Take time to listen to what God is saying to you, and thank Him for all the wonderful things He has done in your life. Thankfulness is the key to living a victorious life free of worry and anxiety.

Day 3

2 Cor. 5:7

For we live by believing and not by seeing.

Set your heart and mind on things above, not on things in the earth. Facing things that are unknown or has an uncertain outcome may cause us anxiety. But if we believe and trust in Jesus Christ, we can share Paul's confidence about eternal life with Christ. We will continue to live. So let this hope give you confidence and inspire you to a life of faithful service in Christ.

Day 4

Prov. 19:21

You can make many plans, but the Lord's purpose will prevail.

We have many plans that we want to accomplish day in and day out. Be sure to consult God with your plans because any plans made outside of God's will is a detriment to your life. We can be so busy doing this and doing that and miss what God is saying and trying to do in our life. This is why prayer is so important, this is when we can commune with the Lord and hear His clear instruction. We should be more like Mary, laying at the feet of Jesus in worship and waiting to hear what God has to say concerning our lives.

Day 5

Prov. 12:25

Worry weighs a person down; an encouraging word cheers a person up.

Anxiety and depression can ho hand and hand. In the text it says, "anxiety in the heart can cause depression." So how important it is to combat worry and anxiety with the Word of God! God's Word speaks life into our bones! The Word becomes alive in our hearts and soul. The song says, "He had made me glad, He has made me glad. I will rejoice for He has made me glad."

Day 6

Isa. 54:17

But in that coming day no weapon turned against you will succeed. You will silence very voice raised up to accuse you. These benefits are enjoyed by the servants of the Lord; their vindication will come from me. I, the Lord, have spoken!

God made a covenant with Noah that He has never broken. Likewise, God made a covenant of peace with the people of Israel. God's promises are Yes and Amen, stand on the promises of God's Word. (1) No weapon that comes against you will destroy you or penetrate. (2) Anything evil someone says about you shall be sent back to the pit of hell from where it came. Allow God's Word and the promises He made to transform your thinking and behaving to live the life that God wants you to live.

Day 7

Matt. 6:25-27

25 That is why I tell you not to worry about everyday life—whether you have enough food and drink, or enough clothes to wear. Isn't life more than food, and your body more than clothing? **26** Look at the birds. They don't plant or harvest or store food in barns, for your heavenly Father feeds them. And aren't you far more valuable to him than they are? **27** Can all your worries add a single moment to your life?

Jesus tells us not to worry about the needs that God promises to supply. Worry may (1) contribute to health problems; (2) difficulty making decisions; (3) Non productivity; (4) relationship stress and how you may treat others negatively; (5) reduce your ability to trust in God. This can be crippling to experience. Here is the difference between worry and genuine concern. Worry immobilizes you, but concern moves you to action.

Join Talitha for devotional hymn chosen to align with this week's focus by scanning this code.

Week 5 - Failure

Lack of success; an act of feeling or proving unsuccessful

Day 1

Ps. 37:24

Though they stumble, they will never fall, for the Lord holds them by the hand.

Our lives are not exempt from failure. At some point in life, we will fail a multiple of times. In Prov. 24:16, it says, "a just man falls seven times and rises up again." The key word is, "a just man." He will not let you be cast out or thrown away. For the Lord will take hold of you and bear you up to sustain you with His support. During times of failure, that's when

God can really show you who He is. He reveals
Himself. God can really show you who He is. He
reveals Himself as Jehova Nissi, my strength, by
banner, my Lord!

Day 2

Ps. 121:1, 2

1 look up to the mountains. Does my help
come from there? **2** My help comes from the
Lord, who made heaven and earth!

This scripture brings to mind that I'm safe in
His arms. You don't have to worry about falling
down or feeling like you've failed. I know it's
hard to face people, and even yourself, when
there's been such high expectations put on
you. This is when you have to look to the hills
which is into the mountains under the heavens,
where my help comes. My help comes from the
Lord, my creator! Here is where we can rejoice.
It's in this place; the reason is God's tender
care for His people. The psalmist speaks of our
everlasting safety to the God of creation. God
owns the world because He made it; nothing
that happens is beyond Him.

Day 3

Ps. 145:14

The Lord helps the fallen and lifts those bent beneath their loads.

God is able to lift us up because His greatness is beyond our understanding. He meets all our daily needs. He is righteous and gracious in all his dealings. He remains near to those who call on Him and He hears our cries, and rescues us. When it seems your burdens are more than you can bear and feel that you are about to fall, turn to God for help. He is there ready to lift you up and bear your burden.

Day 4

Phil. 4:13

For I can do everything through Christ, who gives me strength.

Letting our failures and disappointments dominate us draws us away from God who cares. Yet when everything is good in our lives, we tend to forget God, and forget to be grateful. But whether we lack necessities or live in poverty, we have a lifetime to practice being content. Whatever circumstances we face, Christ is always enough. Paul had a secret in every circumstance, "Christ which strengthens me." Rather than worrying about what he ad or didn't have, he looked to Christ to satisfy his needs. The result wan an unfaltering contentment no matter what his external circumstances were.

Day 5

Mic. 7:8

Do not gloat over me, my enemies. For though I fall, I will rise again. Though I sit in darkness, the Lord will be my light.

We all have sinned and fallen short of the glory of God. This is the confession of the people in saving faith. When you face trials because of your sin, don't be angry with God or afraid that He has rejected you. Instead, turn away from your sin, turn to God, and continue to be patient and obedient.

Day 6

Ps. 73:26

My health may fail, and my spirit may grow weak, but God remains the strength of my heart; he is mine forever.

When we are weak, then we are strong. It is only through our weakness and failures that we can find strength in God. He wants you to trust Him. He wants you to lean on Him and depend on Him. The flesh is weak and corrupt. This is why we need a savior. We cannot save ourselves. God is our portion and His love for His children is eternal.

Day 7

Rom. 5:3-5

3 We can rejoice, too, when we run into problems and trials, for we know that they help us develop endurance. **4** And endurance develops strength of character, and character strengthens our confident hope of salvation. **5** And this hope will not lead to disappointment. For we know how dearly God loves us, because he has given us the Holy Spirit to fill our hearts with his love.

Failure is hard to deal with, it is truly a hard pill to swallow. No one wants to be a failure, but that's just it; failing at something doesn't make you a failure. Paul lets it be known that we can rejoice in our sufferings because it will build your character and patience to deal with life as you go on. There is no success that comes without failure. Your experience produces wisdom and gives you a hope that can't be bought. This hope comes from the love of Christ that dwells on the inside. Hope gives us the faith to keep going by trusting in God to know that all things are working for my good through my love for Christ. He has my hand and with the Lord I will have good success.

SCAN ME

Join Talitha for devotional hymn chosen to align with this week's focus by scanning this code.

Week 6 - Insecure

A feeling of inadequacy; not being good enough. Uncertainty; lack of confidence

Day 1

Prov. 29:25

Fearing people is a dangerous trap, but trusting the Lord means safety.

It is better to have fear and reverence for God who is able to seal your eternal safety. Seeking the approval of men will cost you more than what you are willing to pay. Instead trust in the Lord wo can turn the harm intended by others into good. My safety and security are only found in God's will and His plan for my life.

Day 2

Cor. 3:4, 5

4 We are confident of all this because of our great trust in God through Christ. **5** It is not that we think we are qualified to do anything on our own. Our qualification comes from God.

The older I become, the more I realize that I cannot trust in myself. The bible says, "put your trust in no man." That includes me. It is God who sustains me and keep me in perfect peace when I put my complete trust and confidence in Him to take control of my life. This flesh we have is weak and frail, and when you build up your confidence in it, you will end up very disappointed time and time again. All the Glory and credit goes to God for everything in my life. For every good and perfect thing comes from Him.

Day 3

Ps. 23:1, 5

1 The Lord is my shepherd, I have all that I need. **5** You prepare a feast for me in the presence of my enemies. You honor me by anointing my head with oil. My cup overflows with blessings.

God offers Himself to us as the good shepherd. One that is faithful and trustworthy. David identified his heavenly Father here as His shepherd who provided for his physical, spiritual, mental, and emotional needs. We are all the sheep in God's sight. God will give us everything we need to follow Him. We only need to listen for the voice of our Shepherd. In the midst of temptation when worrying about basic needs, let us pray this Psalm instead and thank God for taking care of us.

Day 4

Jer. 17:7, 8

7 But blessed are those who trust in the Lord and have made the Lord their hope and confidence. **8** They are like trees planted along a riverbank, with roots that reach deep into the water. Such trees are not bothered by the heat or worried by long months of drought. Their leaves stay green, and they never stop producing fruit.

You will always sow what you reap. If what we plant is for God, then we will harvest joy.

Obeying God is an investment with a good return. David said, "Once I was young, and now I am old. Yet I never seen the Godly abandoned" (Ps. 37:25). This is a testament to God's faithfulness to those who put their trust in Him. If we choose to follow Him in every aspect of our lives and obey His Word, He will be faithful through all our struggles. Obedience is better then sacrifice. We may be blessed with prosperity on this earth, or we may suffer like Jeremiah did. Either way, God will not forsake us. He promises that those who trust in God will "be like trees planted along the riverbank, with roots that reach deep into the water." This is the secret to abundant life.

Day 5

1 Pet. 2:9
But you are not like that, for you are a chosen people, you are royal priests, a holy nation, God's very own possession. As a result, you can show others the goodness of God. For He called you out of darkness into His wonderful light.

Today, as we strive to find our place in society, and in the church, this scripture can raise our confidence about our God given significance and capabilities. People often base their self-image on their accomplishments. But the importance of our relationship with Christ transcends our jobs, successes, wealth, or knowledge. We have been chosen by God as His very own and we have been called to represent Him on the earth. Remember, your value comes from being one of God's children, not from what you can achieve. You have worth because of what God does for you, not because of what you do. We can therefore commit ourselves to each other and work together towards God's plan. We know who we are because we know whose we are.

Day 6

Acts 20:32

And now I entrust you to God and the message of His grace that is able to build you up and give you an inheritance with all those He has set apart for Himself.

Paul insisted that he worked with his own hands to provide for his needs and for the needs of those who were with him. Paul argued that this helped him experience the joy of the Lord because, "it is more blessed to give than to receive." Let God build you up that you may be a blessing to others!

Day 7

Rom. 8:30, 31

30 And having chosen them, he called them to come to Him. And having called them, he gave them right standing with Himself. And having given them right standing, He gave them His glory. **31** What shall we say about such wonderful things as these? If God is for us, who can ever be against us?

If God gave His son for you, He will not hold back the gift of salvation: If Jesus gave His life for you, why would He turn around and condemn you. Jesus loves you and He will not withhold anything you need to live for Him. With God on our side, there is no need to be afraid!

*Join Talitha for
devotional hymn
chosen to align
with this week's
focus by scanning
this code.*

Week 7 - Sickness

The state of being ill

Day 1

Mark 5:34

And He said unto her, Damsel thy faith hath made thee whole; go in peace and be whole of thy plague. Your suffering is over.

Damsel, Jesus used this tender word to address this woman, and He noted that her faith made the difference. For it was correctly placed in the Master's hand. Faith itself does not heal. It is the proper object of that faith, Jesus who heals!

Day 2

<u>1 Pet. 2:24</u>

He personally carried our sins in His body on the cross so that we can be dead to sin and live for what is right. By His wounds you are healed.

The purpose of Christ bearing our sins is that we might live to please Him. Jesus paid the price for our sins that we, being dead to sin, should live unto righteousness. For our healing is in His stripes!

Day 3

<u>Ps. 147: 2-4</u>

1 The Lord is rebuilding Jerusalem and bringing the exiles back to Israel. **2** He heals the brokenhearted and bandages their wounds. **3** He counts the stars and calls them all by name.

We need to remember that the work that's done in the hearts of men and in our lives is God's work, and He will see that it is accomplished. Let God heal your heart. God's principal work is always within the human heart.

Day 4

Matt. 4:23

Jesus traveled throughout the region of Galilee, teaching in the synagogues and announcing the good news about the kingdom and he healed every kind of disease and illness.

Jesus' miracles of healing show His concern for wholeness. He can heal us, not just from physical sickness, but from spiritual sickness as well. There is no sin too great or too small for Him to handle.

Day 5

Matt. 9:35

Jesus traveled through all the towns and villages of that area, teaching in the synagogues and announcing the Good News about the Kingdom. And he healed every kind of disease and illness.

Jesus' ministry during this time on earth was extensive. It was also holistic, meaning that he healed body, mind, and spirit. He did not just call people to repent of sin, he also compassionately healed them of all their sickness. Jesus ministered to their spiritual and physical needs, and He wants to the same for you and me.

Day 6

<u>Prov. 16:24</u>

Kind words are like honey, sweet to the soul and healthy for the body.

Pleasant words are as a honeycomb. The Hebrew word for honeycomb is also used in Ps. 19:10, 11, with regard to the Word of God. The children of Israel saw honey as a healthy food as well as a sweater. It would commode positive, healthful effects. God's Word is like the honeycomb that gives me health to my bones, and sweet to the soul.

Day 7

<u>3 John 1:2</u>

Dear friend, I hope all is well with you and that you are as healthy in body as you are strong in spirit.

As a responsible child of God, you should not neglect nor indulge yourself but care for your physical needs and discipline your body so that you are at your best for God's service. We ought to be good stewards over our bodies and know that we are ambassadors for Jesus Christ. This text suggests a sense of wholeness, a quality of life that one enjoys when following God's precepts.

Join Talitha for devotional hymn chosen to align with this week's focus by scanning this code.

Week 8 - Unpretty

Unattractive, or unappealing to look at

Day 1

Prov. 31:30

   Charm is deceptive, and beauty does not last, but a woman who fears the Lord will be greatly praised.

   Favor, which could be translated, "graciousness," like beauty can deceive us about the true nature of someone's character. But if a woman fears the Lord, that is trustworthy and more worthy of praise than physical comeliness.

Day 2

1 Pet. 3:3, 4

3 Don't be concerned about the outward beauty of fancy hairstyles, expensive jewelry, or beautiful clothes. **4** You should clothe yourself instead with the beauty of a gentle and quiet spirit, which is so precious to God.

Being beautiful in the eyes of the world does not mean that we are beautiful in the eyes of God, or even our spouses. No amount of beauty can cover a bitter angry, or disagreeable attitude. It is good for believers to groom ourselves and dress appropriately, but we must not spend too much of our time trying to be attractive on the outside. If we focus on our appearance, we misuse our time, energy, and money. External beauty fades, but a beautiful character will never fade, so character is what believers should spend time cultivating.

Day 3

2 Cor. 4:16

That is why we never give up. Though our bodies are dying, our spirits are being renewed every day.

Paul concentrated on experiencing the inner strength that comes from the Holy Spirit. Renew your commitment to serving Christ. Don't forsake your external reward because of the intensity of today's pain. Your temporary weakness allows the resurrection power of Jesus Christ to strengthen you moment by moment.

Day 4

Eph. 2:10

For we are God's masterpiece. He has created us anew in Christ Jesus, so we can do the good things He planned for us long ago.

We are God's masterpiece (work of art, workmanship). He alone masterminds our salvation. He works powerfully and creatively in us. He is the potter, and we are the clay. If God considers us His masterpiece, we dare not treat ourselves or others with disrespect or as inferior work.

Day 5

Ps. 139:14

Than you for making me so wonderfully complex. Your workmanship is marvelous – how well I know it.

He is the God who knows. He knows everything that has happened and will happen. He understands all of nature perfectly. In fact, He knows everything there is to know. He is omniscience.

Day 6

<u>1 Sam. 16:7</u>
But the Lord said to Samuel, "Don't judge by his appearance or height, for I have rejected him." The Lord doesn't see things the way you see them. People judge by outward appearance, but the Lord looks at the heart.

Samuel could see only Eliab's outward appearance, but the Lord saw his heart. When choosing a friend, employee, or spouse, do not judge by appearance. Even the prophet Samuel was deceived by Eliab's appearance. Ask God to give you insight into the person's character. We should focus on developing hearts that trust God, so that God will choose to use us for His purposes.

Day 7

1 Cor. 3:16

Don't you realize that all of you together are the temple of God and that the spirit of God lives in you?

We must understand that we, the Body of Christ, are a unified assembly ("all of you together are the temple of God and the spirit of God lives in you"). We are not to see ourselves as a collection of competing interests or independent individuals. Believers are unified in God. Women tend to compete with one another and try to compare ourselves to one another, but this is not of God. We are all unified in God, a body jointly fit together. Let God build you up in your most holy faith and take time to strengthen your ties to your fellow Christians in the love of Christ.

Join Talitha for devotional hymn chosen to align with this week's focus by scanning this code.

Week 9 - Bitterness

Anger and disappointment at being treated unfairly; resentment

Day 1

John 16:33

I have told you all this so that you may have peace in me. Here on earth, you will have many trials and sorrows. But take heart because I have overcome the world.

When the pressures of life tend to take over your life and you are overcome with bitterness of heart, just remember that Jesus Christ has overcome the world. He knows just how you feel. He knows the affliction and distress you're going through. Jesus will never leave you or forsake you. Now, God never promised that life would be easy for you, but just know that trials and difficulties will pass away. God's grace is sufficient and given in abundance to those who trust in Him through the hard times in life.

Day 2

Ps. 51:10

Create in me a clean heart, O God. Renew a loyal spirit within me.

Bitterness is never good for anyone. When you feel overwhelmed with bitterness, first confess it to the Lord. Confession leads to forgiveness. The results of forgiveness are a clean heart, a renewed spirit and a right standing relationship with God. When the sin of bitterness is revealed, we are compelled towards seeking His healing and forgiveness. This allows us to escape the hold that bitterness can have on our hearts, repent, and humble ourselves to a new spirit from the Lord. When you put all this together, there is a great cause for joy on our part. It takes that which is wrong in our life and makes it right.

Day 3

Prov. 28:13

People who conceal their sins will not prosper, but if they confess and turn from them, they will receive mercy.

Admitting to being wrong is so hard for people to do. I truly admire people who can openly admit their mistakes and sins. That characteristic requires a different condition of the heart. I call it the "God factor." Once we recognize the bitterness in our hearts, we must confess. Our confession must be made aloud, out loud to the Lord, and to our sisters and brothers in Christ. When people know how we really feel, then they can pray and encourage us to overcome the bitterness that is inside. To learn from having bitterness, you need to admit it, analyze it, and make adjustments so it doesn't happen again. Everyone makes mistakes, but only fools repeat them.

Day 4

Eph. 4:26

And don't sin by letting anger control you. Don't let the sun go down while you are still angry.

Unresolved anger can easily become a dangerous bitter root in our hearts. Paul tells us to deal with our anger immediately in a way that builds relationships instead of destroying them. We must be completely honest with ourselves when we are angry and pray and ask the Lord for strength. Don't let the day end before you begin to work on reconciling your relationship.

Day 5

Col. 3:13

Make allowance for each other's faults and forgive anyone who offends you. Remember, the Lord forgave you, so you must forgive others.

Forgiving others starts by remembering how much God has forgiven us. Ponder on that for a second. The Lord instructed His people to forgive not only when they feel like it, but out of obedience to Him. It is difficult to forgive someone who has wronged you, but realizing God's infinite love and forgiveness for you can help you love and forgive others. Forgiveness doesn't remove the consequences, but it frees us from the pain and burden of bitterness.

Day 6

Eph. 4:31

Get rid of all bitterness, rage, anger, harsh words, and slander, as well as all types of evil behavior.

When you want to deal with bitterness, just get rid of it. It will reake havoc in your life and home like smelly trash. It will infiltrate every area of your life and eventually you won't even realize it. You will get used to the smell. Anyone who comes to visit you will notice it right away. So handle it right away by confessing and repenting of the bitterness in your heart so the Lord can bring you to a new and better place of life in Him.

Day 7

Eph. 3:17-19

17 Then Christ will make this home in your hearts as you trust in Him. Your roots will grow down into God's love and keep you strong. **18** And may you have the power to understand, as all God's people should, how wide, how long, how high, and how deep His love is. **19** May you experience the love of Christ. Though it is too great to understand fully. Then you will be made complete with all the fullness of life and power that comes from God.

In Christ we lack nothing, have nothing to lose, and have nothing to fear. No matter what the situation is that brought on bitterness, God's love is deep, it reaches to the depths of bitterness. When you feel isolated, remember that you can never be lost to God's love. God sent His son to die for you. This love of God also wants the best for you in this life.

SCAN ME

Join Talitha for devotional hymn chosen to align with this week's focus by scanning this code.

Week 10 - Anger

A strong feeling of annoyance, displeasure, or hostility

Day 1

James. 1:19, 20

19 Understand this, my dear brothers and sisters. You must all be quick to listen, slow to speak, and slow to get angry. **20** Human anger does not produce the righteousness God desires.

It is time to get rid of all the filth and evil in your lives, and humbly accept the word God has planted in your hearts, for it has the power to save your souls. I'm a person that talks too much and listen too little. This is a communication to others that we think our ideas are more important than theirs. James tells us to reverse this process. Outrage has become the normal reaction to anyone who disagrees with us. We should become angry because others are being hurt. We should not become angry when we fail to win an argument. Selfish anger never helps anyone. This is why we must be swift to hear, slow to speak, and slow to wrath.

Day 2

Prov. 14:29

People with understanding control their anger, a hot temper shows great foolishness.

Pray that God will help you control your quick temper. A quick temper can be like a fire that is out of control. Anger divides people. It pushes us into hasty decisions that cause bitterness and guilt. God can help us to conquer selfish anger through humility and repentance.

Day 3

Ps. 103:8

The Lord is compassionate and merciful, slow to get angry and filled with unfailing love.

If God dealt with us according to our sins, no one could stand before Him. He is merciful and gracious to help us forgive us even when we are undeserving. God is faithful, so we should be faithful by putting our complete trust in Him in every area of our lives.

Day 4

Eccles. 7:9

Control your temper, for anger labels you a fool.

For anger rests in the bosom of fools. Anger is a destructive flood, working all kinds of havoc in our lives. It often leads to a bitter life with strife. It disrupts and disunites families and may even lead to murder.

Day 5

Prov. 22:24, 25

24 Don't befriend angry people or associate with hot-tempered people, **25** or you will learn to be like them and endanger your soul.

Remember the saying, "You are the company you keep," or "birds of a feather flock together?" People tend to become like those they spend a lot of time with. Unfortunately, negative characteristics can rub off on you. The Bible tells us to be cautious in who you choose as companions. Choose wisely to spend time with people who have qualities that are Christ like and that you would like to develop in your life.

Day 6

Eph. 4:29, 30

29 Don't use foul or abusive language. Let everything you say be good and helpful, so that your words will be an encouragement to those who hear them. **30** And do not bring sorrow to God's Holy Spirit by the way you live. Remember, He has identified you as His own guaranteeing that you will be saved on the day of redemption.

We should never push away the Holy Spirit of God. If we would remember that the one who lives in us is God's own Spirit, we should be much more selective about what we think, read, watch, say, and do. The Holy Spirit within us is a guarantee that we belong to God.

Day 7

Rom 12:19

Dear friends, never take revenge. Leave that to the righteous anger of God. For the scriptures say, "I will take revenge; I will pay them back," says the Lord.

Paul says to befriend them who deeply hurt you. Don't try to give them what they deserve. Why do we forgive our enemies? Forgiveness breaks the cycle of retaliation and leads to mutual reconciliation. Repaying evil for evil hurts you just as much as it does your enemy. Even if your enemy never repents, forgiving him or her will free you of a heavy load of anger and bitterness.

Join Talitha for devotional hymn chosen to align with this week's focus by scanning this code.

Week 11 - Laziness

The quality of being unwilling to work or use energy; idleness

Day 1

1 Cor. 9:24, 27

24 Don't you realize that in a race everyone runs, but only one person gets the prize? So run to win! **25** All athletes are disciplined in their training. They do it to win a prize that will fade away, but we do it too for an eternal prize. **26** So I run with purpose in every step. I am not just shadowboxing. **27** I discipline my body like an athlete, training it to do what it should. Otherwise, I fear that after preaching to others, even I might be disqualified myself.

We must put in the hard work in order to get the reward. As Christians, our living is not in vein. We are running toward our heavenly reward. So train diligently like an athlete; your spiritual progress depends upon it. Self-discipline requires an honest look in the mirror to examine your strengths and weaknesses, with emphasis on the latter. When it comes to laziness, pray for God's help to redirect that weakness into strength. The prize or crown however, is the reward for endurance and suffering for the cause of Christ.

Day 2

Heb. 6:11, 12

11 Our great desire is that you will keep on loving others as long as life lasts, in order to make certain that what you hope for will come true. **12** Then you will not become spiritually dull and indifferent. Instead, you will follow the example of those who are going to inherit God's promises because of their faith and endurance.

An athlete trains hard and runs well, remembering the reward lies ahead. The certainty of our hope keeps us from becoming lazy. Hope requires both an attitude of expectation for what God will do and confidence that we will have eternal life with new bodies on a new earth, as he has promised.

Day 3

Phil. 2:12, 13

12 Dear friends, you always followed my instruction when I was with you. And now that I am away, it is even more important. Work hard to show the results of your salvation, obeying God with deep reverence and fear. **13** For God is working in you, giving you the desire and the power to do what pleases Him.

Don't allow laziness to ruin your present or your future. We must focus our attention and devotion even more on Christ so that we won't be sidetracked. God gives us the desire and the power to do what pleases Him. We find the secret to a renewed life when we submit to His will and let Him work in and through us. There is always a reward to hard work. The Word and "hard work" is used to speak of digging silver out of silver mines. Salvation can be compared to a huge gift that needs to be unwrapped for one's thorough enjoyment. Paul encourages the Philippians to develop and work out their salvation, but not to work for their salvation.

Day 4

<u>1 Cor. 6:19, 20</u>

19 Don't you realize that your body is the temple of the Holy Spirit, who lives in you and was given to you by God? You do not belong to yourself, **20** for God bought you with a high price. So, you must honor God with your body.

Jesus bought us with a price – with His death. Jesus Christ paid the cost to redeem us from slavery to sin. Honor God with your body every day. Go where He wants you to go; do what He wants to do. Take action to let the Lord know that your faith is real in Him. Faith without works is dead. Now is the time to move, get up, seek Him, pray, walk and not faint, and run and not grow weary. God honors your faithfulness.

Day 5

<u>Prov. 19:15</u>

Lazy people sleep soundly, but idleness leaves them hungry.

Don't allow laziness to steal what God has for you. Slothfulness can come in and cause you to sleep your way out of experiencing the promises of God. When we fail to experience God's promises to us Don't allow, our soul is left without the fuel/nutrition, it needs to remain strong. Don't allow your soul to suffer hunger. Just know that your labor is not in vain; In all labor there is profit.

Day 6

James 4:14, 15 How do you know what your life will be like tomorrow? Your life is like the morning fog: It is here a little while, but then it's gone. What you ought to say, *Is if the Lord want us to, we will live and do this or that.*

Don't be deceived into thinking that you have all this remaining time to live for Christ, to enjoy loved ones, or to do what you know you should. Live for God today! Then, no matter when your life ends, you will have fulfilled God's plan for you.

Day 7

John 9:4 We must quickly carry out the tasks assigned us by the one who sent us. The night is coming, and then no one can work.

We must carry out the tasks assigned us by Jesus and not get distracted. We must focus on them as Jesus did.

Join Talitha for devotional hymn chosen to align with this week's focus by scanning this code.

Week 12 - Worthless

Having no real value or use

Day 1

Matt. 6:26

Look at the birds. They don't plant or harvest or store food in barns, for your heavenly Father feeds them. And aren't you far more valuable to Him than they are?

This is to tell us that God will definitely bless us in due time as we are much more important than the animals which He looks after as well. You ought to believe in God as your savior and provider, knowing His amazing love is available to transform your life and fulfill His promises to you.

Day 2

<u>Jer. 1:5</u> I knew you before I formed you in your mother's womb. Before you were born, I set you apart and approved you as my prophet to the nations.

It's so important to know that the call of God on your life has been determined by God from before conception. Jeremiah understood that God knew him and called him. We must understand the true meaning of the word 'knew,' as it is used in this way. It refers to an intimate knowledge that comes from relationship and personal commitment to God. God, who formed you in your mother's womb, hears each person individually and understands all your worries and concerns.

Day 3

<u>Eph. 2:10</u> For we are God's masterpiece. He has created us anew in Christ Jesus, so we can do the good things He planned for us long ago.

We are God's masterpiece. He works powerfully and creatively in us. He uses us as is canvas. If God considers us His masterpiece, we dare not treat ourselves or others with disrespect or an inferior work. This verse clearly emphasizes our worth and value as God's work of art, and it implies that our worth is not based on our achievements or abilities, but on the fact that we were created by a loving and all-powerful God.

Day 4

Is. 43:4 Others were given in exchange for you. I traded their lives for yours because you are precious to me. You are honored, and I love you.

   Since we belong to Him and bear His wonderful name, we must remember that He is always with us. We are never beyond God's love and concern no matter how small or insignificant we may feel, and we can trust that He is always with us and watching us.

Day 5

Prov. 31:10 Who can find a virtuous and capable wife? She is more precious than rubies.

   The woman of Proverbs 31 is more valuable than rare jewels because of her wisdom and her skill at living responsibly, productively, and prosperously. Do not see her as a model to imitate in every detail. Your days are not long enough to do everything she does. I see her instead as an inspiration to be all you can be. The Proverbs 31 models for both women and men a way of living that brings fulfillment and contentment. Her life of work and love flows from godly wisdom.

Day 6

2 Cor. 5:17 This means that anyone who belongs to Christ has become a new person. The old life is gone; a new life has begun!

The Holy Spirit gives us new life, and we are not the same anymore. We are recreated, new creations living in vital union with Christ. We have a new covenant, a new perspective, a new spirit, a new community. The new nature must be cultivated or nurtured by spiritual decisiveness to grow in Christ. We must not revert to putting on the old suit of the former life; rather, we much continue to grow in this new life.

Day 7

Jer. 29:11 For I know the plans I have for you," says the Lord. "They are plans for good and not for disaster, to give you a future and a hope.

God knows the future and His plans for us are good and full of hope. As long as God who knows the future, directs our agendas/plans and goes with us as we fulfill His assignments, we can have boundless hope. This does not mean that we will be spared pain, suffering, or hardship. That is a guaranteed part of life in this sinful world. But it does mean that God will see us through to a glorious conclusion.

Join Talitha for devotional hymn chosen to align with this week's focus by scanning this code.

Going Forward

This 12 week devotion could be repeated or used as a launch pad for further study and connection between life and the Word of God.

Acknowledgements

I am so grateful for my son Daniel, he is such a blessing to my life. I am a better woman because of him. I'm thankful to my parents, William & Barbara Davis who have always been there to challenge me, and push me to be the woman of God that desires me to be. I love you immensely. Thank you to my Pastor, Kevin Matthews & First Lady Malissa Matthews for being such a beam of light and investing God's Word into my Spirit. You are truly a blessing from the Lord. Thank you to all my family, friends and church family for all your love and support. I love you with the love of Christ!

About the Author

Talitha C. Davis is the CEO of Damsel Arise Creations, LLC; founder of Damsel Arise, and Author of the Powerfully Inspiring book "Damsel, Arise To The New You"

Talitha Davis is also a Minister and Health & Wellness Coach; her passion is to please

God in all things as well as to help others to live a life of Optimum Health in Body, Mind, and Spirit. Talitha Davis is truly born to serve others through Inspiration, Encouragement, and Empowerment through Christ.

About the Business:

Damsel Arise is a Holistic Ministry that spreads the message to women and young girls to be who God created you to be, women of God's Purpose.

Damsel Arise is a movement and a lifestyle that empowers and teaches women how to lead by example for the next generation.

Website: www.damselarise.org

Email: info@damselarise.org

Connect with Me:

Instagram: @iamdamselarise
TikTok: @iamdamselarise
Twitter: @iamdamselarise

Made in the USA
Middletown, DE
07 November 2023

42004018R00056